MENAI BRIDGE

A Pictorial History

by

John Cowell

Published by the Menai Bridge Community Heritage Trust

Copyright © Menai Bridge Community Heritage Trust, 2014

All rights reserved. No part of this publication may be reproduced or transmitted in any form or by any means, electronically or mechanically, including photocopying, recording or any information storage or retrieval system, without prior permission in writing from the publishers

First published in 2014

ISBN 0 9518592 6 9

FOREWORD

As chairman of Menai Bridge Community Heritage Trust it gives me great pleasure to introduce this lovely book illustrating the history of Menai Bridge town (Porthaethwy). The Trust is very grateful to John Cowell for producing this book and for allowing us to market it for Trust funds.

John Cowell is a well-known and popular local author and historian who is also a long-standing supporter of the Trust's work, contributing significantly to our archive. The illustrations and information in this book complement much of the material in the Menai Heritage exhibition in Canolfan Thomas Telford Centre (the former National School). In the near future our intended move to the restored warehouse at Prince's Pier on the waterfront will enable us to expand the displays and interpretive material.

I thoroughly recommend this book to everybody who has connections with, or an interest in, Porthaethwy/Menai Bridge. It will bring back memories for local residents and may have some surprises for visitors to the town.

Bob Daimond
Chair, Menai Bridge Community Heritage Trust

Canolfan Thomas Telford, Menai Bridge, tel. 01248 715046
info@menaiheritage.org.uk, www.menaiheritage.org.uk

PREFACE

This book is a modest attempt to provide a brief introduction to the main events that have helped to develop Menai Bridge from the small scattered community at the beginning of the nineteenth century to the pleasant residential town of today. Hopefully it will also stimulate interest in what Menai Bridge was like in former days and to recapture the nostalgia of an age which has gone for ever.

Most of the illustrations are taken from picture postcards from 1902 to 1914. This was the golden age of postcards when they were sold everywhere and sent by everyone, preserving for us that lost atmosphere of an unhurried way of life when pleasure steamers arrived at the pier, roads were devoid of cars and chapels full on Sundays. The Britannia Bridge has been included because it played an important part in the history of the Menai Strait, and it features prominently in the Telford Centre Museum.

Facts have been derived from contemporary sources, including the Minute Books of the Menai Bridge Urban District Council and its sub-committees, Census Returns, business directories and the *North Wales Chronicle.* I have also relied on information from the late Herbert Anthony's excellent book *Menai Bridge and its Council* (1980) as well as from other local publications. Any errors of fact arising from the misinterpretation of sources are entirely mine.

Money is expressed in its original form of pounds, shillings and pence, leaving the reader to make the conversion of one shilling (written as 1/-) = 5p and 20 shillings = £1 In order to make a true comparison of values, one should take into account the enormous drop in the purchasing power of the pound over the years. As a rough-and-ready guide, based on the Retail Price Index, it would now cost £94 to buy the same basket of goods and services that £1 would have bought in 1900, £60 in 1931 and £20 in 1960.

I acknowledge with profound gratitude the assistance received from Julie Stone who gave her time freely to scan the illustrations, to Warren Kovach who kindly oversaw the preparation of the book for publication, to Paul Smith, to the courteous and helpful staff of the Anglesey Archives, Llangefni, to John Hughes for sharing his inexhaustible knowledge of Menai Bridge, and to Helen Butterworth and Gerwyn James for providing information from their own specialised areas of research. I am also very grateful to the following who kindly entrusted me with their original photographs and postcards, and for allowing me to reproduce them in the book:

John Hughes, pp. 44, 60, 72, 78, 80, 83 and 105.
Maureen Parry Williams from the collection of her father, the late Alf Morris,
pp. 100, 101, 102, 104 and 109.
Those on pp. 43, 46, 58, 59, 66, 108 and 112 are from the Heritage Trust archive.

Every effort has been made to trace the original owners of other photographs used in the book but where this has not been possible I can only apologise for any unintentional breach of copyright.

Menai Bridge   John Cowell
October 2014

INTRODUCTION

The early development of Porthaethwy stems from its position on the post road from London to Dublin. Prior to 1718 the Irish mails were carried across the treacherous Lavan Sands between Aber and Beaumaris, and from thence on the old line of road to Holyhead. But for most of the seventeenth century the ordinary traveller, in order to avoid the dangers of the tidal sands, had gone through Bangor and across the Porthaethwy Ferry before following the direct road to Holyhead via Penmynydd to join the old post road from Beaumaris at Hirdrefaig near Llangefni. And as the post could not be delayed it is almost certain that the postboys would also have taken this direct route whenever the tide was in.

Most travellers journeyed on horseback as roads were completely unsuited to wheeled traffic. The road leading to the ferry was in a perilous state until a new road was opened over Penmaenmawr in 1772 to improve the connection between Chester and Bangor, and coaches started running along it. In 1785 mail coaches were introduced to carry the Irish mail to Holyhead by way of Chester but in 1808 the Post Office transferred the mail via Shrewsbury along the recently opened Capel Curig road, linking Bangor to London via both Chester and Shrewsbury. This was, for North Wales, the beginning of the coaching age. The two roads now converged on the ferry, and Porthaethwy became increasingly important as the recognised crossing place for two London mail coaches and a number of public stage coaches, bringing with them fashionable passengers who rested and refreshed themselves in the George Inn on the Bangor side of the Strait and at the Cambria Inn at Porthaethwy.

The Act of Union of 1801 made good communications essential as Ireland was ruled from Westminster. Government officials needed to be in close touch with Dublin and Irish MPs had to travel regularly to London. Supported by the Post Office they agitated for Government assistance to improve the Holyhead Road where the most dangerous parts were in Anglesey, resulting in constant delays and frequent accidents. In response to these complaints the first of a succession of parliamentary committees was appointed in 1810 to examine the whole question. Local turnpike trusts had neither the funds nor the skill to cope with a national highway so Thomas Telford was commissioned to make a complete survey of the road and then to improve it by widening, straightening, levelling, resurfacing and diverting it, including the building of a completely new road across Anglesey. His culminating achievement was the Menai suspension bridge, built in 1826 in order to avoid the delay in crossing the Strait by ferry. This was the third attempt to solve the engineering problem involved. Previous plans in 1783-5 for a wooden drawbridge and in 1801 for a cast-iron bridge of three arches had been defeated, chiefly by opposition from Caernarfon whose merchants believed that a bridge would obstruct its sea trade with Liverpool.

A new era had dawned in the history of communications between London and Dublin. The mail coach journey between London and Holyhead had been shortened from 41 hours in 1815 to 27 hours, including the time taken for meals and for change of horses no fewer than 27 times. And the 3½ hour journey across Anglesey was reduced to 2 hours 12 minutes. Better roads brought more coaches and more people.

The opening of Telford's bridge was a great stimulus to the growth of Porthaethwy, or what slowly became known as Menai Bridge. People moved there to live and work, shops opened up, trade developed and lodging houses sprang up to cater for visitors. In 1801 it was little more than a scattered village of 55 houses and a population of 263 with almost 50 per cent engaged in agriculture. By 1831 the population had increased to 479 with 42 more houses built and only 16 per cent now working on the land. In the next twenty years the population almost trebled to 1,243 due mainly to the settlement of outsiders. In 1851 only 36 per cent of the population were born in the town, the remaining two-thirds having moved there to live, 50 per cent of whom came Caernarfonshire and other parts of Anglesey in search of work. And in order to accommodate the incomers 172 new houses had been built. The birth of Menai Bridge had begun.

Much of this growth was due to the foresight and entrepreneurial skills of the remarkable Davies brothers (John, Robert and Richard) whose father, Richard, had been a successful storekeeper in Llangefni. With a shrewd eye for business he saw the potential for his sons to engage in commerce in the developing town of Menai Bridge after the opening of Telford's bridge two years earlier. They began by buying and selling timber and iron before acquiring a fleet of fine ships, carrying slates and emigrants to America and returning with timber and guano. The business flourished and the firm became the town's largest employer, providing regular employment for both skilled and unskilled labour in the timber yard, the saw mill, the roller mill, the wholesale grocery warehouse and on the wharf.

The inauguration of a steamer service between Liverpool and Menai Bridge in 1822 was a further significant stage in the development of the town. It brought thousands of English tourists to view the bridge during its construction and to marvel at it after completion. The only alternative method of travel was by coach (the railway did not arrive until 1848) but this was expensive, slow and uncomfortable. In favourable weather conditions the voyage by steamer was made in five hours, less than half the time taken by coach. In the years that followed intense rivalry between ship-owners led to a daily service during the summer months, bringing well-to-do visitors to the town. In order to land them safely a stone pier was built by the St George Steam Packet Company about 1835 so that the steamers could tie alongside at all times of the tide. The steamers also brought more road traffic to connect with sailing times, with coaches running from Holyhead, Amlwch and Caernarfon.

Before Llandudno, Rhyl and Colwyn Bay had emerged as popular watering places, Menai Bridge became a fashionable resort. Hotels were built, boarding houses opened up and inns proliferated. In 1853 the *North Wales Chronicle* boasted that "Menai Bridge is becoming a large and thriving place, and during the summer months is frequented by hundreds of English visitors". But when the holiday season ended the town slumbered. To many, the winter months meant unemployment and hardship, with dependence on charity from local benefactors who gave generously to those in distress.

Living conditions in the town, particularly in areas away from the tourists, were deplorable, revealing the deep inequalities within late Victorian society. There was no adequate water supply, few cottages had privies, household refuse was left in the open and streets remained uncleaned. Many of the working class houses had serious defects and overcrowding was common. But with the appointment of Improvement Commissioners in 1879, who in turn were superseded five years later by a Local Board of Health, public health and sanitation slowly began to improve. By-laws were introduced to ensure that streets were kept clean, slaughter houses inspected, earth privies installed and drains disinfected.

An elected Urban District Council came into being in 1895 and continued the work of improving the town. A reservoir was built at Tyddyn To, roads were regularly maintained, pavements constructed for pedestrians, refuse was collected and disposed of and a bathing place established at Carreg-yr-Halen. Streets were named, re-named and numbered and were lit by gas from the Llyn-y-Felin gasworks.

Slater's *Commercial Directory* of 1895 recorded that Menai Bridge had been "considerably extended of late, and will doubtless in a short time vie with other watering places on the Welsh coast". The population had increased to 1,600, a new middle class was emerging and new shops were opened to cater for their needs. Slater listed over 50 shops including 18 grocers, 4 drapers, 4 shoemakers, 4 coal merchants, 3 confectioners, 3 butchers, 3 fruiterers, 2 chemists, 2 ironmongers, 2 milliners, 2 china & glass dealers, 2 bakers, a watchmaker, a tobacconist & hairdresser and a bookseller. There could well have been more as the accuracy of early directories is somewhat doubtful through poor techniques of enumeration. It is possible that shops outside the High Street were not included.

The Town Council soon realised that the economic future of Menai Bridge lay entirely in tourism. It had tremendous potential as no other town could compete with the sightseeing value of the Strait and the two bridges but it had fallen behind the other north Wales coastal towns. A wide promenade leading to a new pier became essential. Financed by a loan of £14,000 from Cardiff Corporation these were completed and officially opened by David Lloyd George in 1904. The investment was a resounding success. The next ten years were the golden age of tourism and during the summer months Menai Bridge flourished.

The general acceptance of half-day Saturdays and the extension of paid holidays resulted in more leisure time for the masses. Helped by an increase in real wages and an improvement in living standards families were now able to visit the seaside, either as day-trippers or for a week's holiday. Outings were also arranged by clubs, societies and Sunday schools, all leading to an upsurge in demand for pleasure cruises from a wider public. Each Edwardian summer saw 300,000 passengers carried on the Liverpool & North Wales Steamship Company's four vessels plus an unknown number brought by the Isle of Man steamers. Llandudno was the favourite stopping-place but Menai Bridge also shared in this boom with an average of 30,000 visitors landing at the pier each summer, together with many more arriving by rail. Visitors were well catered for as local people took full advantage of the commercial possibilities offered by holidaymakers. Apart from the two main hotels (the Anglesey Arms and the Victoria) a number of public houses provided accommodation along with the 21 apartments and boarding houses listed in Slater's *Directory*. There were also 6 restaurants and several tea rooms.

The short Edwardian era, on which most of this work is based, saw more social and technological changes than in the whole of the previous hundred years. A national system of elementary education had become established, paid for out of the rates, and children were being medically examined at school. Literacy was steadily increasing and newspaper sales rising. Streets were lit by electricity, the telephone came into gradual use and letters reached their destination the next morning. Holiday traffic was booming, the sale of bicycles growing and betting on football was spreading. Birth rates and infant mortality were falling and the expectancy of life was increasing. Old age pensions were introduced for those aged seventy while unemployment benefit and sick pay for the needy laid the foundations for the Welfare State. It was an age of innovation and progress. Technology was developing rapidly with the invention of the wireless (radio), the gramophone and the box camera while silent films were shown in the New Hall. But the greatest change which took place was the arrival of motor transport, the visible symbol of a new age.

Yet, people still lived in a class-ridden society in which everyone knew his or her place. Towering above the rest of society were the immensely wealthy Pagets of Plas Newydd and the Bulkeleys of Baron Hill, both of whom had property in Menai Bridge. Below them was the middle class with its blurred boundaries and wide range of incomes within it. At its upper end were families like the Prices of Cadnant, the Verneys of Rhianfa and the ship-owning Davies family, all of whom lived comfortably, kept servants, sent their sons to public school and whose wives did very little work. In the "middling" area were professional people like doctors, lawyers and bankers while in its lower reaches were 'white collar' workers like teachers, clerks and shopkeepers who by definition "worked with their brains rather than their hands".

Roughly 80 per cent of Menai Bridge people belonged to the working class. Although some improvement had taken place since Victorian times, most employees were overworked, underpaid and frightened of the sack. Working conditions were deplorable. A 55-hour week was standard and earnings were depressingly low. The average weekly wage was just over £1, a sum which might have proved adequate for a newly-married couple but could cause severe hardship to families with several children, plunging them into poverty and debt. In some occupations it was even lower. Agricultural labourers were paid as little as 15/- while gas workers in Menai Bridge went on strike for an extra shilling.

Roadmen employed by the Anglesey County Council received 17/- a week but this could be increased to £1 for a twelve-hour day. Women were harshly exploited. A parlourmaid could be hired for £12 a year 'all found' while female shop assistants earned as little as 15/- for a 70-hour week. It was not until 1911 that they became entitled to a half-day holiday each week, and as late as 1914 the Shop Assistants Union was campaigning for a 60-hour week. And, of course, women were denied the vote until they were partly enfranchised in 1918. Yet not all workers were as badly paid. Skilled craftsmen and senior clerks, forming an elite group at the top of the working class, earned in the region of £2 a week.

Large sections of the working class lived well below the poverty line, and surveys showed that 90 per cent of those who died during the Edwardian era left nothing at all. At the very bottom of society, below the working class, were the destitute who through unemployment, illness or the death of the breadwinner were unable to make ends meet. Those who could prove real need were given outdoor Parish relief in exchange for which they had to break stones for repairing roads or perform other labouring tasks. The Town Council also helped by opening a subscription list for the unemployed out of which they were paid 18/- a week for repairing and painting the pier.

Old age was another major cause of poverty despite the introduction of Lloyd George's means-tested State pension in 1909. For the small minority who were fortunate enough to survive until the age of seventy a sum of 5/- a week was paid to single persons and 7/6d to married couples provided that any other income did not exceed 10/-. But as the pension alone was insufficient to live on and wages too low to save enough for old age, most men continued working for as long as they could. In 1911 for example there were 37 Menai Bridge men over the age of seventy, 25 of whom were still in employment. Those unable to do so, and with no other resources, were forced to seek the grudging help of the Parish. And the prospect of entering Bangor workhouse, followed by a pauper's burial, was viewed with horror by the elderly. There was further help in the social measures introduced in 1911, again by Lloyd George, whereby compulsory health insurance provided workers (but not their families) with medical attention and a weekly sickness benefit of 10/-.

Apart from tourism the main sources of male employment were in William Roberts's timber yard and roller mill, the wholesale grocery warehouses of John Edwards and Hugh Williams, local stone quarries, the Cadnant woollen mill and on nearby farms. Others worked as gardeners and handymen for the well-to-do, on the railway and as dock labourers on the wharf. There were very few 'collar and tie' jobs. Women were not so fortunate. Because of social convention and the lack of job opportunities only one-third of Menai Bridge women of working age were in paid employment in 1901, 50 per cent of whom were in domestic service. The only other significant categories of female employment were dressmaking, sick nursing, teaching and retailing.

Little material exists about the domestic lives of ordinary Menai Bridge people during the Edwardian era but we do know that religion was important to them. A Royal Commission Report on Religion in Wales, published in 1911, concluded that 70 per cent of the town population were members of Nonconformist chapels with another 13 per cent churchgoers. Furthermore, 251 children under the age of 15 went to Welsh Sunday school plus 51 to St Mary's church. The figures should, however, be interpreted with caution as the Report does not reveal the average attendance at Sunday services, the real indicator of people's faith. The middle classes were the most stalwart supporters of church and chapel and they felt it important to set an example to the lower classes. Richard Davies and his sons were staunch Calvinistic Methodists and their workers would also have attended chapel, some because they genuinely believed in its message, others through loyalty to their employers.

Although the chapels preached thrift and temperance, the public house was the chief form of recreation for working men, tempting them to escape from the grim reality of life. The Temperance Movement, having a policy of total abstinence from intoxicating drink, opened a cocoa house in Bridge Street as an alternative attraction to the public house but it had little effect in reducing the consumption of alcohol. This was only achieved in 1914 under the Defence of the Realm Act which restricted opening hours, weakened the strength of beer and imposed a steep rise in excise duty.

The common language of Menai Bridge people was Welsh. The Welsh Language Census of 1901 indicated that 88 per cent of the town population aged three and over spoke Welsh (55 per cent today) compared with 72 per cent in Beaumaris, 97 per cent in Llangefni and 92 per cent in the county as a whole. One in five was enumerated as a monoglot Welsh speaker, and among those aged 65 and over the figure was as high as one in four.

By the end of the Edwardian years many improvements had been made by the council since its inception in 1895. The town had developed into an attractive seaside resort with a promenade and a new pier, benches had been placed on the waterfront, public toilets built, street lights converted from gas to electricity and improvements made to the water supply. A Fire Brigade had become established and new council offices built in Dale Street.

Despite the social inequalities of the time much had been achieved and there was a feeling of optimism for the future until the outbreak of war in August 1914 brought everything to an abrupt halt. Inspired by patriotism and the adventure of war, scores of young Menai Bridge men flocked to the recruiting centre to volunteer with no idea of the horrors awaiting them in the killing fields of

France and Flanders. The war dragged on for four years, resulting in the most fearful casualty list ever known with Menai Bridge losing over 30 of its bravest young men. Those left at home had a difficult time dealing with war conditions when real wages were being eroded by inflation. Food shortages led to supplies being controlled by a sub-committee of the Town Council before rationing came into force in 1918 and continued for another three years. Those who depended on tourism for their livelihood suffered badly as the Liverpool pleasure steamers were requisitioned by the Admiralty during the four years of war. Few people were taking holidays, and those who did came by train. When conscription was introduced in 1916 women moved into new areas of employment traditionally reserved for men. Refugees driven out of Belgium by the German invasion arrived in Menai Bridge in October 1914, and in gratitude for the town's hospitality they built the promenade along the foreshore from Carreg-yr-Halen to Church Island. It was completed in 1916 and became known as the 'Belgian Prom'.

After the war the housing shortage became acute. "Homes for heroes" had been a universal promise during the General Election of 1918 and local authorities were ordered to build more houses. Menai Bridge Council responded positively by building 16 State subsidized houses on the gasworks field in 1919, named Rhyd Menai, at an average cost of £1,084 each and let to working class families for 9/- per week for parlour houses and 6/6d for non-parlour ones. The council's building programme continued with 12 houses in Brynaethwy in 1930, named Bro Hyfryd, 10 in New Street the following year and 14 in Bron Fedw (Mount Street) and Well Street from 1934, having first condemned 32 insanitary cottages in Dale Street, Wood Street, Dew Street and Well Street where overcrowding was common. Prior to 1914 only the middle class benefited from houses with running water and inside toilets but after the Town Council's revolutionary house-building programme new tenants saw a vast improvement on the dwellings they replaced, with proper sanitary facilities, electric lighting and a garden.

The hectic post-war boom in which jobs were plentiful and earnings high was followed in 1921 by a severe depression which brought mass unemployment to areas largely dependent on traditional heavy industries on which the country's prosperity had once relied. Although Menai Bridge was less affected than these areas it still suffered. Business activity declined and in 1931 as many as 9 per cent of the town's working population were unemployed. There was some relief during the summer season but holidaymaking never seemed to reach the heights of the pre-war boom. The Town Council did everything possible to assist the unemployed. Contractors were instructed to use local labour on its house-building programme, on the widening of Dale Street and on the construction of the bowling green in 1934. Other projects which helped those out of work were the conversion of the former Iorwerth House café in Water Street into the War Memorial Institute, the re-building of the New Hall into a cinema and the laying out of a football pitch on the old slateworks yard.

Other planned improvements were halted by the Second World War which brought 460 evacuees from Liverpool to escape from possible air raids as Merseyside was an obvious danger zone. This figure included 325 schoolchildren and their teachers, together with 100 mothers with young children. The difficulties of accommodating such vast numbers were immense but the billeting officers, helped by members of the WVS and other volunteers, succeeded in housing them all with local families and in empty houses commandeered by the council. By the following January many of the evacuees had returned home as the expected bombing had not materialised during the period of the 'phoney' war but the start of the heavy blitz on Merseyside in August 1940 brought a second wave of evacuees, all of whom were welcomed with warmth and kindness. By April 1943, when air raids had virtually ceased, they had all left.

The visible signs of war were everywhere in the town. ARP wardens patrolled the streets, Fire Guards kept vigil at night and the Home Guard manned road blocks after dark. The incessant drone of enemy bombers was heard overhead as they made for Liverpool at night and sirens were sounded. Menai Bridge escaped the bombing but a high explosive bomb and several incendiaries were dropped on the outskirts of Llandegfan, fortunately without damage or loss of life. Pleasure sailings ceased and the Admiralty took over the pier. Road signs were removed to confuse an enemy agent, rumours of spies abounded and railings were removed for salvage. Identity cards were issued and the carrying of gas masks became a habit. A blackout was enforced from sunset to sunrise, streets were unlit at night and cars had their headlights masked. Rationing was imposed on food, clothes and petrol, and there were shortages of all kinds. Many goods disappeared from the shelves and beer often ran out in the pubs. Children fared badly as well. Toys vanished from the shops and sweets were severely rationed. Workers were taxed as never before to finance the costs of war. Purchase Tax was introduced in 1940, Income Tax gradually raised and the duty on drink and tobacco was doubled. Women were mobilized for the first time in history and there was plenty of work for those left behind in jobs vacated by men. Family life was completely disrupted with wives separated from husbands, children from fathers and mothers from sons.

After Germany's surrender in May 1945 the country gradually returned to peacetime conditions and there was much to look forward to in Labour's social reform programme after Atlee's landslide victory in the 1945 General Election in which it was committed to provide a free National Health Service, children's allowances, a comprehensive social insurance scheme and a stable level of employment. But those trying to adjust to civilian life faced a housing crisis. There was an enormous demand for council houses in Menai Bridge from newly-married couples and from returning servicemen who no longer wished to live in rooms or with their in-laws. The Town Council, fully aware of the problem, embarked on an ambitious house-building programme. In 1948 a total of 44 council houses were built in Trem Eryri, followed in stages by several more in Tyddyn To and Tyddyn Mostyn, as well as flats for the elderly at Maes-y-Coed in 1970.

As living standards improved land was made available for private dwellings. From 1953 an estate of houses and bungalows was built on 15 acres at Cae Tros Lon, 57 bungalows at Maes-yr-Hafod, 14 at Gors Goch, several houses at Tyddyn Isaf and dozens more on smaller sites such as Fron Heulog and Y Glyn, as well as on individual plots. A number of public buildings were also erected, notably a new fire station, a branch library, a new primary school and the David Hughes Secondary School (transferred from Beaumaris). Furthermore, the University's School of Ocean Sciences had been expanded, providing not only employment but support for local businesses. As Menai Bridge developed so did the amenities. Two tennis courts were provided alongside the football field in 1952 and a cricket pitch at Tyn-y-Caeau in 1968. A new bus station was built in the Wood Street area in 1967 and two large car parks: on the Waun in 1967 and another with access from the Square three years later. Other major schemes included a new cemetery behind the Holyhead Road in 1956, the reconstruction of the pier in 1969 and a refuse tip at Penhesgyn in 1970 to be shared initially with Beaumaris and the Aethwy District Council.

The Liverpool pleasure steamers resumed sailing in 1946 after release by the Admiralty and continued to bring day-trippers and holidaymakers to Menai Bridge but numbers were falling. People preferred the sandy beaches and seaside amenities which Llandudno and Rhyl could provide, while the growth of family motoring contributed to the decline. At the end of the 1962 season it was announced that the Liverpool & North Wales Steamship Company had gone into voluntary liquidation. This came as a severe blow. Menai Bridge had lost its tourist trade, and no more holidaymakers from Liverpool would pour off the steamers to spend money in the town.

In 1974, as part of local government reorganisation, Menai Bridge Urban District Council was replaced by a Town Council, by which time the town had become a 'travel to work' area and a desirable place in which to live. In the fifty years to 1951 the population had increased by a modest 19 per cent but during the last fifty years it has risen by 47 per cent to a total of 3,375 while the number of houses has almost doubled to 1,600, helping to transform the Menai Bridge which our ancestors knew into the dormitory town of today.

The Church of St Tysilio, standing on Church Island, is an early example of Celtic Missionary work. Tysilio, a monk from Meifod, established a sanctuary on the island and a tiny church was erected there about the year 630 AD. The present church was probably built at the beginning of the fifteenth century and was described by Angharad Llwyd in 1832 as "A small edifice remarkable for the bleakness of its situation". It was later modernised and is now well cared for.

After the opening of the suspension bridge in 1826 thousands of English tourists flocked to see it, the vast majority travelling by steamer as coaching was slow and expensive and the railway did not appear until 1848. One such visitor recorded his experience in a letter to his cousin in August 1829: "The Bridge is upwards of 1700 feet in length and is suspended by iron chains and so high above the water that large vessels may sail under it. I send you a sketch of the bridge"

The bridgemaster's house during the early 1900s, occupied by Alfred Thorpe and his family, showing his children selling refreshments on a table outside. Thorpe was responsible for the day-to-day running of the bridge, its maintenance and the collection of tolls from the two booths, one at each end. Note the four chains running through the upper part of the house. These ran through deep tunnels at the back of the property and were anchored in tons of concrete.

The toll booth on the Caernarfonshire side where tolls were collected from all users of the bridge. Pedestrians paid a penny while charges for coaches and carriages varied with the number of horses used. With the coming of motor transport, buses were charged 3/6d and cars 1/9d but in 1935 these were reduced to 1/3d and 6d respectively. The large notices refer to the Motor Act of 1903 which made registration and licence plates compulsory, and to the weight restriction on the bridge.

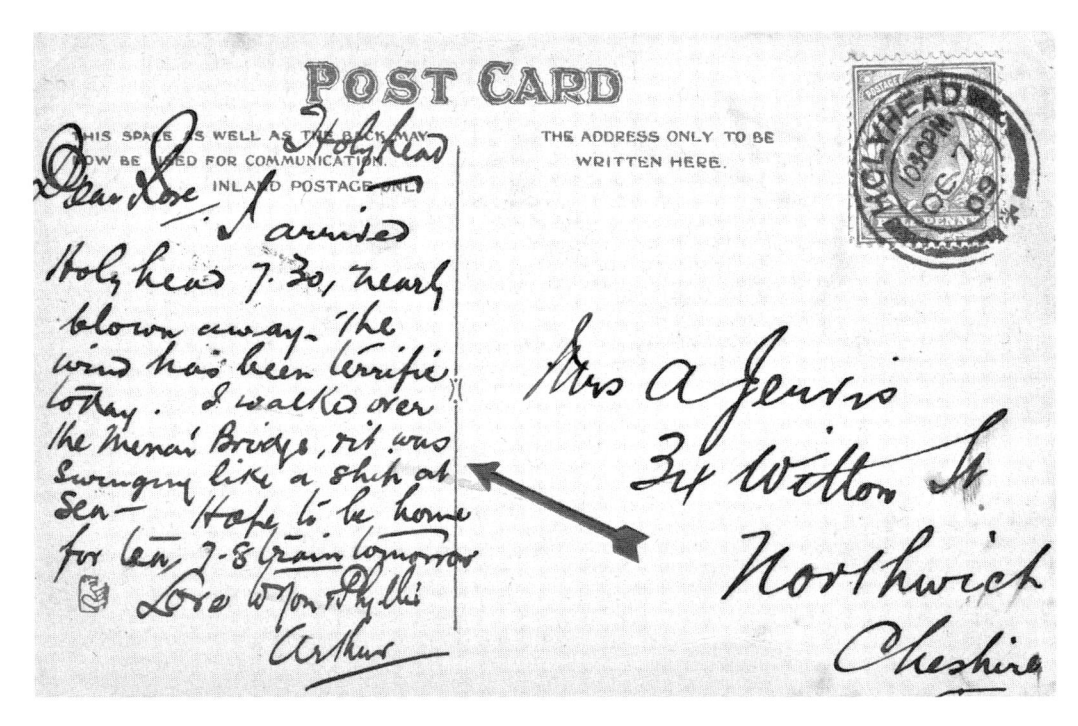

The suspension bridge occasionally suffered damage by strong south-westerly gales that funnelled down the Menai Strait. A particularly severe one occurred in 1903 when the carriageway became disconnected from the two stone piers, causing it to move to and fro. Six years later it again swung freely as indicated by the writer of this postcard: "The wind has been terrific today. I walked over the Menai Bridge and it was swinging like a ship at sea"

Before the advent of motorised wagons it was not unusual to see livestock being walked across the suspension bridge, as indicated by this postcard of 1905. The sheep, on which a toll was charged, were probably on their way to be sold in the Mona Road market place as a cyclist on foot threads his way past. The centre span was for the use of pedestrians until new walkways were added on each side of the bridge during its reconstruction in 1938-39.

Holding up the traffic. The driver of this car had time to stop and take a photograph of his vehicle as he crossed the suspension bridge on 25th March 1913, exactly a month after it was first registered. The car was a 20 h.p. two-seater Ford, owned by a Henry Pratt of Crewe. Notice the bald tyres which were a normal feature on early cars. Punctures were a constant problem on some of the untarred roads of the day, and tyres needed replacing every thousand miles or so.

PAINTING THE MENAI BRIDGE.   10606.

The suspension bridge required constant maintenance, including regular painting, but there was no health and safety assessment for these painters balancing precariously on the chains without even harnesses, hard hats or high-viz jackets. And the unknown brave photographer was unlikely to have had any protection either as he operated his camera from an even greater height. The postcard is undated but was probably published in the 1930s.

M.93. TELFORD'S SUSPENSION BRIDGE, MENAI STRAITS, N.WALES. A.W.H.

A weight limit of 4 tons was imposed on all vehicles crossing the suspension bridge to prevent undue strain on its fabric. It was rigidly enforced during the early 1920s with weighbridges installed at each end. Passengers on loaded buses were made to walk across the bridge before being picked up on the other side as shown on this postcard of 1937 with passengers walking alongside their bus on the Anglesey side. The house on the left was occupied by the tollkeeper.

The reconstruction of the suspension bridge in 1938-39. By the late 1930s it became apparent that Telford's masterpiece was no longer suitable for motor transport so in 1938 Dorman Long & Co. were commissioned to modernize and strengthen it. The stonework was still sound and was left untouched, apart from widening the archways, but a new road deck was constructed, the ironwork renewed and the four chains replaced by two. It was a remarkable feat of engineering.

HMS *Conway*, a Merchant Navy Cadet School, was evacuated from the River Mersey to a safe anchorage near Bangor pier in 1941 in order to escape the heavy blitz on the Liverpool docks. In April 1949 she was towed to new moorings near Plas Newydd where a shore establishment was provided by the Marquess of Anglesey in order to accommodate more training places as a result of increasing post-war demand. This photograph shows her passing under the suspension bridge.

On the morning of 14th April 1953 the *Conway* left her moorings at Plas Newydd to be towed to Birkenhead for a refit but in negotiating the Swillies Channel she met the spring flood tide and a sudden north-westerly wind. One of the tug's tow ropes parted and she ran aground near the suspension bridge with her hull badly strained and buckled and little hope of refloating her. The wreck then mysteriously caught fire and burned furiously for 18 hours before breaking up.

A carrier goes about his normal business on this short but well-used stretch of road outside Ceris Lodge near the Caernarfonshire end of the suspension bridge in 1907. It led to Menai Bridge railway station where horse-drawn carts collected goods for short haul deliveries and hackney carriages picked up holidaymakers from the trains. A private driveway from the lodge led to 'Ceris', the imposing waterside home of John Robert Davies of the wealthy ship-owning family.

An early motor accident on the suspension bridge in October 1906. A 12 horse-power Wolseley (EY 4), owned by Samuel Chadwick of Haulfre, Llangoed, and driven by his chauffeur, collided with the toll collector's booth on the Bangor side of the bridge. The car can be seen on the road leading to Menai Bridge station where it was towed by horse to be transported by rail to the Wolseley Motor Company's factory as there was no local garage capable of repairing the damage.

Menai Bridge railway station was built on the Bangor side of the Strait in 1858 as the main line had bypassed the town. It had an imposing stone building, an island platform, a further 'down' platform for Caernarfon traffic and a goods yard. It became a very busy station. The LNWR timetable of 1908 shows that 38 trains stopped there each weekday, 19 in each direction. The station was closed to passengers under the Beeching axe in 1966 and for freight two years later.

BRITANNIA TUBULAR BRIDGE, LOOKING N.W.

ROBERT STEPHENSON, ENGINEER.

One of a series of postcards issued by the LNWR Company in 1905. Stephenson's bridge was the first to be built using a tubular design without supporting chains, a revolutionary idea in bridge building. With its opening in 1850 the train was able to make the entire journey from London to Holyhead in only 9½ hours, a considerable improvement on the mail coach time of 27 hours. The great days of coaching were now well and truly over.

Two lions guard the entrance to the Caernarfonshire side of the Britannia Bridge on a postcard of 1918. Another pair, carved by the sculptor John Thomas out of limestone from Penmon quarry, appears on the Anglesey side. Each of the four lions measures 25 feet in length, over 12 feet in height and carved out of 80 tons of stone. Sadly today they are hidden from the view of thousands of motorists who cross the bridge each day.

Soldiers of 'A' Company of the Anglesey Volunteer Reserves pose for the camera before taking up guard duties on the Britannia Bridge during 1917. They were men too old for or otherwise excused from the regular army. The Irish troubles had threatened to flare up into civil war in 1914, and fearing reprisals against the postponement of the Home Rule Bill, the entrances of both bridges were manned by the reservists. The expected sabotage never materialised.

An attractive billhead of 1840. In 1828 Richard Davies, seeing the growth potential of Menai Bridge, leased some land on the waterfront where he built a warehouse and a timber yard. With his three sons he established a thriving business there, importing groceries from Liverpool and timber from America. The two parts of the business were run as separate entities, the wood yard trading under the name William Roberts and the wholesale grocery warehouse as John Edwards.

A decorative billhead of Hugh Williams, a wholesale grocer of Bodfair Stores, Cadnant Road, for goods purchased in 1894. The business had been established in 1886 in the face of stiff competition from the much larger concern of John Edwards. The invoice shows the trading practice of granting credit at this time. Three months was normal, with a discount of 2½% given for settlement within one month and 1¼% in two months. And bills were always paid in cash.

Liverpool and Menai Bridge.

THE POWERFUL AND FAST SAILING NEW IRON STEAMER
CAMBRIA,
Captain JOHN HUNTER,

WILL sail from the Menai Bridge on TUESDAYS, THURSDAYS, and SATURDAYS, at Nine in the morning, and will leave George's Pier, Liverpool, on MONDAYS, WEDNESDAYS, and FRIDAYS, at Eleven in the morning.

☞ At the Menai Bridge apply to Mr. Robert Humphreys, Jun., at Liverpool to

PRICE & CASE.

On SATURDAY next, the 23rd instant, the "CAMBRIA" will sail for BEAUMARIS and BANGOR at a Quarter before Four, Afternoon, and will leave BANGOR on MONDAY next, the 25th, at Six, Morning, precisely; and will continue to leave LIVERPOOL every alternate SATURDAY, and BANGOR every alternate MONDAY, at the same hours, until further notice.

FARES FOR THE ROUND.
Cabin........................ 7s. 6d.
Steerage.................... 4s. 0d.

At the Menai Bridge, apply to Mr. R. HUMPHREYS, Jun.; at Liverpool, to PRICE and CASE.

19 May 1845

THE CITY OF DUBLIN COMPANY'S Splendid and Powerful NEW IRON STEAMER the
"PRINCE OF WALES,"
Of 400 Tons Burthen, and 200 Horse-power,
W. H. WARREN, R. N., Commander,
(Built expressly for the Station,)

Has commenced plying between Menai Bridge, Bangor, Beaumaris, and Liverpool, and will continue for the Summer on the days and hours following—namely:—

From Menai Bridge, MONDAYS, WEDNESDAYS, and FRIDAYS at 10 o'clock morning.

From George's pier-head, Liverpool, TUESDAYS, THURSDAYS and SATURDAYS, 11 o'clock, morning.

Cabin fare .... 6s.
Steerage do. .... 2s. 6d.

Children under 12 years, Cabin 3s. Steerage, 1s.6d.

Further particulars may be had on application to Mr. E. W. Timothy, or Messrs. R. and H. Humphreys, Menai Bridge; Mr. John Hughes, Ship-agent, Carnarvon; Mr. Robt. Pritchard, Post-master, Bangor; Mr. T. Byrne, Post-master, Beaumaris; or to Mr. J. K. Rounthwaite, at the Company's Office, 24, Water Street, Liverpool.

Menai Bridge, 20th April, 1846.

28 April 1846

North Wales Chronicle

A regular packet service between Liverpool and Menai Bridge was established as early as 1822 and in the years that followed sailing notices appeared regularly in the *North Wales Chronicle* and in the Liverpool papers. The early vessels were wooden paddle steamers of some 200 tons, equipped with engines of 60 to 70 horse-power and rigged to carry sail as well. In good conditions the voyage was made in about five hours, less than half the time taken by coach. Fares were 10/- for a cabin and 5/- on deck. Horses were charged a guinea and carriages 10/6d a wheel. Breakfast and dinner were available on board as well as wines and spirits "of the best quality".

There was intense competition for the lucrative tourist business, with several ship-owners entering the service, each claiming superior speeds, greater safety and lower fares. The largest one was the City of Dublin Steam Packet Company whose greater resources enabled it to put larger vessels on the route, the best known of which were the *Prince of Wales* and the *Prince Arthur*, sailing on alternate days three times a week in each direction during the summer months, as indicated on the notice of 1846 shown on the opposite page. The company also extended the pier at Menai Bridge by adding a pontoon for the convenience of passengers.

This patchwork service lasted until 1891 when, after a series of amalgamations, the Liverpool & North Wales Steamship Co. was established, and for the next seventy years it gained the virtual monopoly of the excursion service, bringing thousands of holidaymakers and day-trippers to Menai Bridge in its fleet of fine steamers to spend in the pubs, shops and cafes. But at the end of the 1962 season the company went into voluntary liquidation, bringing to a close 140 years of local maritime history.

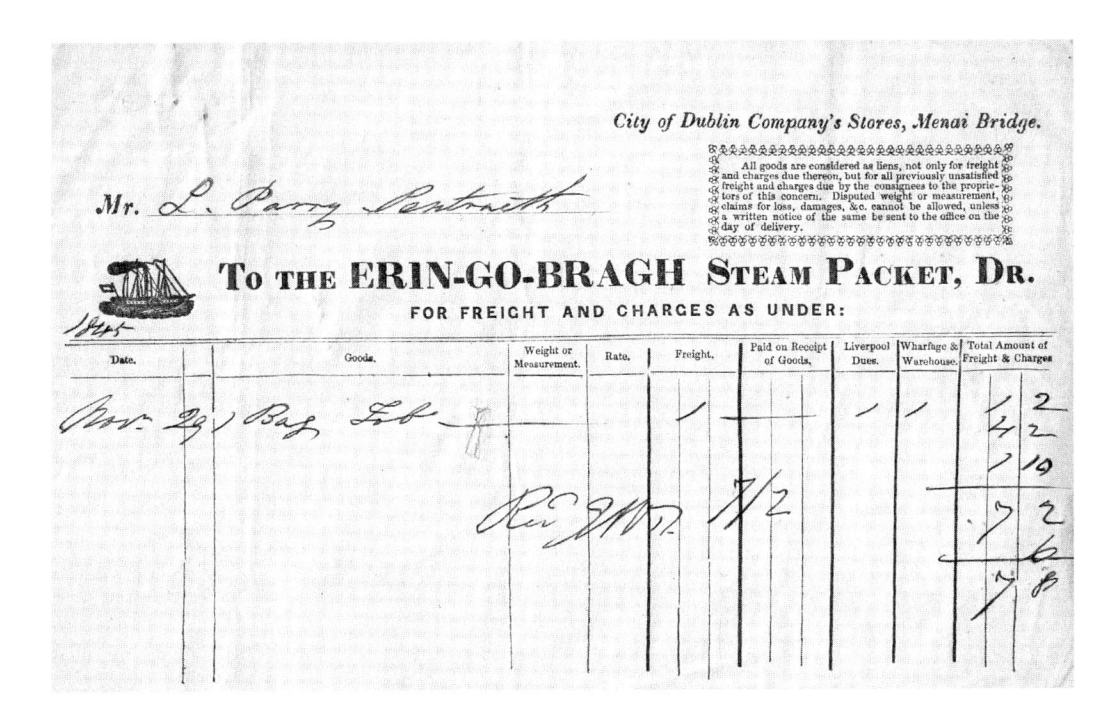

A consignment note of the City of Dublin Steam Packet Company issued from the firm's office in Menai Bridge in 1845 for a bag of tobacco carried from Liverpool on the *Erin-go-Bragh*. She was the first iron paddler to be used on the north Wales route and, like most pleasure steamers, she carried freight as well as passengers. Lewis Parry, the consignee, a Pentraeth grocer, paid a wharfage charge of 1d for having his goods stored in the company's warehouse before collection.

The old stone pier was built by the St George Steam Packet Company about 1835. By the 1890s, as larger pleasure steamers were being used on the excursion service, it proved to be inadequate to cope with the increasing number of passengers arriving daily. It gradually fell into disrepair so Prince's Pier was used instead by the shipping companies. A replacement was essential so a new one, authorised by Act of Parliament, was built and officially opened by Lloyd George in 1904.

The *Prince of Wales*, a small paddler at Prince's Pier during the early 1900s. The stone wharf was built by Richard Davies around 1837 for unloading timber from America, and during the 1860s part of it was leased to the City of Dublin Steam Packet Company who constructed an iron girder bridge to link the quayside to a pontoon in order to improve passenger facilities. This was called Prince's Pier, and by association the stone wharf became known by the same name.

A family group, staring fixedly into the camera, rest on Bonc Mostyn c.1898, having probably arrived from Liverpool on the *St Elvies* paddle steamer seen berthed at Prince's Pier. She was a fine looking vessel with a passenger capacity of 991 and operated on the north Wales service from 1896 to 1930. She was also used for cruises around Anglesey and weekly excursions from Menai Bridge to the Isle of Man where passengers were allowed 2½ hours ashore.

The promenade in the course of construction on Bonc Mostyn in 1903 after it became apparent that the town's economic future lay entirely in tourism. A wide promenade leading to a new pier became essential to attract holidaymakers and to compete with the other north Wales coastal resorts of Llandudno, Rhyl and Colwyn Bay. It was built by Isaac Evans, a local man, for £1,564 and officially opened, along with the new pier, in September 1904

The new promenade during the summer of 1905. The galvanised pavilion in the distance was erected at a cost of £154, paid for by an interest-free loan from one of the town councillors. Its main purpose was to provide a concert room, hired out for 10/- per evening plus 5/- for the use of the piano, but could not be used to provide entertainment on Sundays. It was also used for meetings of the Town Council and, in 1913, film shows were provided there three times a week.

Guarding the pier gates. A toll of a penny was charged for admission to the pier in order to cover its annual expenditure. Numbers varied with the season but in 1911 over 32,000 people paid to promenade its length, collected by the pier assistant seen outside his kiosk. The building next to the Liverpool Arms, marked with a cross by the writer of this 1907 postcard, was the warehouse of John O. Edwards, a wholesale grocer and competitor of the other (and larger) John Edwards.

Visitors on the promenade gather around the confectionary stall of the Williams family of nearby Beach House (see page 77) in 1910. Stallholders, who had to be residents of Menai Bridge, were charged a rent of £1.10s for the summer season but no Sunday trading was allowed. Vending machines were also authorised by the council, and by 1914 there were eight in operation together with five stalls selling refreshments and souvenirs.

St Tudno (II) arriving shortly after the opening of the new pier in 1904. Launched in 1891 with accommodation for 1,061 passengers and given the same name as the vessel she replaced, she sailed daily from Liverpool each summer before being sold in 1912. The pier was a popular attraction for those who simply wanted to stroll along it to take the air. Others used it to take short pleasure trips by up to 19 local boat owners licensed by the council to carry passengers.

Passengers disembarking from the *La Marguerite* in 1905. She was the largest excursion steamer of her time, measuring 341 feet in length and registered to carry 2,077 passengers, with every facility provided for their comfort. She left Liverpool at 10.45 in the morning from 1904 to 1925, calling at Llandudno, Beaumaris and Bangor before returning home at 7.30 in the evening, a round trip of 98 miles. The close-up view of the paddle-box gives some idea of its size.

"La Marguerite," the Pier, Menai Bridge

Passengers pouring off the *La Marguerite* in August 1905. They arrived at 2.40 pm and were allowed an hour ashore to spend money in the shops, tea-rooms and pubs. During the Edwardian era an average of 30,000 passengers landed at Menai Bridge each summer, and in the month of June 1905 official figures show that an average of 415 holidaymakers arrived each day. The council was paid one penny by the shipping company for each passenger landing on the pier.

28th September 1925. *La Marguerite* arriving on her farewell voyage. There were touching scenes on her final departure with rockets fired in salute. The pier was crowded with a cheering throng of people waving handkerchiefs, including local children who had been given time off school. Beaumaris also gave her a good send-off with the town band playing 'Auld Lang Syne' whist at Llandudno thousands of people joined in singing 'Farewell my own true love'.

The *Snowdon* arriving in Menai Bridge from one of her regular pre-war excursions from Llandudno to Caernarfon where passengers were allowed two hours ashore. Occasionally she ventured further afield to Blackpool and the Isle of Man. The *Snowdon* was specially built for the excursion business in 1892 with a speed of 14 knots and comfortable accommodation for 462 passengers. Apart from the war years she sailed each summer until the end of the 1931 season.

THE "ST. TUDNO" AT MENAI BRIDGE PIER.

St Tudno (III) in 1953. She had replaced the *La Marguerite* in 1926 and sailed on the north Wales service each summer until her owners went into voluntary liquidation in 1962. She was a fine-looking ship with a length of 329 feet and a speed of 19 knots. Certified to carry 2,493 passengers she was one of the largest pleasure steamers under the British flag. Her spacious accommodation included three dining rooms, lounge bars, a ladies salon and private cabins.

ST. SEIRIOL PASSING UNDER MENAI SUSPENSION BRIDGE

St Seiriol (II) passing under the suspension bridge in July 1935 on one of her cruises around Anglesey, a distance of 150 miles and advertised as "the finest one day sail in Britain". She left Liverpool at 10.15 am, calling at Llandudno and Menai Bridge before arriving back at 9.10 pm. She was a smaller version of her sister-ship *St Tudno,* being 279 feet long. Internally she was an almost exact replica except that she was registered to carry 937 fewer passengers.

St Trillo, a motor vessel 150 feet in length with accommodation for 568 and designed to cater for short sea excursions between Llandudno and Menai Bridge, as well as to Amlwch, and for afternoon and evening cruises. Originally named *St Silio* when acquired in 1936 she was re-named *St Trillo* after returning from war service in 1946. Unlike her sister-ships she had two funnels, and although smaller in size her accommodation was comfortable.

Celebrating Queen Victoria's sixty years on the throne on 22nd June 1897. Local butcher John Jones leads a procession on horseback down Bridge Street, accompanied by the Menai Bridge brass band. It was a grand social occasion with crowds enjoying the official holiday. Although she had long years of seclusion during widowhood, the Victorians had a strong feeling of affection for the Queen, and the celebrations brought together all sections of the population.

Sports at the Waun field as part of the festivities to mark the Queen's Diamond Jubilee in June 1897. It attracted hundreds of spectators including many ladies who can be seen lining the field in their finery. There were no women's events in the programme as female involvement in sports was thought to be 'unladylike'. Children were presented with Jubilee mugs and enjoyed a tea party in the New Hall while the aged poor were cared for in Capel Mawr schoolroom.

A large crowd in festive mood gathers in the High Street in July 1907 to welcome Edward VII and Queen Alexandra as they passed through the town on their way to Baron Hill from Bangor where the King had laid the foundation stone of the University College building. Despite the shortcomings of his private life, people had a great affection for Edward as he had been a popular Prince of Wales, and since his coronation he had changed the whole appeal of the monarchy.

Waiting for the arrival of the Carnival parade in 1930. The star of the picture is undoubtedly the awe-inspiring figure of the local policeman, the reassuring face of authority who was there to direct traffic and to keep an eye on any mischief-makers. The premises on the left show two chemists (Roberts's Medical Hall and Parry Jones's Apothecaries Hall), a tobacconist, Parry's motor garage, Goodwin's glass & china shop and the Prince of Wales Vaults.

This view of the High Street in 1907 indicates that the horse ruled the road. It was the only form of transport for the carriage of goods to and from the railway station and for the household delivery of coal and milk. Although cars were beginning to appear at this time the motor lorry failed to replace the horse-drawn wagon until after the First World War. Notice that the cart had stopped in the middle of the road. It was quite usual for carriers to park as the mood took them.

This High Street scene is typical of the arrival of a visiting photographer as children gaze curiously at the camera in August 1905. The shop on the immediate right is Mona House, one of four drapers in the town, and shows a range of ready-made clothes in the window. Mass produced ready-to-wear clothes in the latest styles had gradually being introduced and their cheapness brought them within the means of all but the poorest members of society.

A typical view of the lower High Street in 1906, previously known as Beaumaris Road. Children playing in the distance have the road to themselves as motor traffic was still in its infancy. The shops on the left were those of WE Parry, cabinet maker and upholsterer (No.33), David Roberts, tailor (No.35), Arthur Davies, 'purveyor of meat' (No.37), Winstanley & Son, watchmaker & jeweller (No.45) and HT Owen's cycle shop (No.47). Nant Terrace is seen in the distance.

Susan Goodwin poses for the photographer outside her glass & china shop at No.13 High Street in the early 1900s. The shop with the canopy a few doors away was the Star Supply Stores, a branch of one of the largest food retail chains in Britain and one of the first to be established in Anglesey. Its success was based on economies of scale, with bulk-buying and a rapid turnover. Goods were branded and pre-packed with prices prominently displayed.

Herbert's Railway Supply Stores at No.8 High Street was one of 14 grocers in the town before 1914. Its tightly packed window display was arranged to attract customers as competition was becoming keener after the arrival of the Star Supply Stores with its improved techniques of selling. Herbert's shop was open all hours, orders were delivered and credit offered to trusted customers. The assistants in their clean white coats give the impression of efficiency and service.

Rees Roberts's pharmacy in 1908. With no National Health Service at the time, many people relied on 'quack' remedies and proprietary medicines for a host of ailments, calling the doctor only as a last resort. In addition to preparing his own potions Roberts would have stocked Beecham's Pills, Venos Cough Cure, Vapex Inhalant, Milk of Magnesia, Fynnon Salts, Bile Beans, Holloway's Pills, Clarke's Blood Mixture, Gripe Water and Seigel's Syrup.

High Street, Menai Bridge

A quiet summer's day in 1905 as a lady does her shopping and a group of girls stand chatting in the road. All provide a clear picture of the fashions of the day, being conventionally clothed from top to toe. Edwardian women would never be seen out of doors without a hat because of the widespread belief that a tanned skin was a sign of commonness. It was only after the war that hemlines rose steadily and make-up used, reflecting the growing emancipation of women.

SQUARE & WATER STREET, MENAI BRIDGE.

The Square being used in 1910 for what was originally thought to be its proper purpose: a place to stand and talk and where children could play safe in the knowledge that they would not be run over. Motor traffic had not even begun to affect town life. The solitary street lamp was lit by gas supplied by the local gas works. It was not until 1913 that the town's streets began to be lit by electricity.

August 1914. The age of motoring arrives and it grew steadily throughout the Edwardian era. In 1903, the first year of compulsory registration, only 13 new cars had been registered in Anglesey but by 1914 the figure had increased to 409, bringing them within the budget of professional people and successful businessmen. These early cars were generally unreliable so owners would have made full use of Luther Jones's garage on the right for both repairs and petrol.

A large crowd in the Square celebrating the end of war in November 1918, a war which changed everything and affected everyone. Britain alone lost three-quarters of a million dead with hardly a home untouched by the tragedy. And Menai Bridge itself lost over 30 of its finest young men. The war did not end for the parents, widows or children of those killed, nor for the broken lives of those badly wounded in the trenches. For them the war lasted far longer than the conflict itself.

Water Street, formerly named Packet Road, on a postcard published about 1907 but posted much later in 1922. There were four pubs in this short length of road at this time. At the end of the terrace on the left was the Avondale Restaurant which had been built on the site of the former Ship Inn at the turn of the century. The building on the right (the present War Memorial Institute) was Iorwerth House, former refreshment rooms, which housed Pringle's confectionary shop.

BULKELEY ARMS HOTEL. MENAI BRIDGE. Propr. JT.AVERILL.
EXCELLENT ACCOMMODATION FOR COMMERCIALS & TOURISTS. MOTOR GARAGE & STABLING
EVERYTHING OF THE BEST.

The Bulkeley Arms shown on a postcard of 1910 published by JT Averill, the proprietor. The Bulkeley was one of several pubs in the town providing accommodation for both holidaymakers and travelling salesmen. It also offered "Good stabling", equivalent to today's "Parking in rear of premises", as well as facilities for motorists. The horse-drawn hackney cab was on one of the three designated cab stands in the town, the others being the pier and the suspension bridge.

A quiet scene in Bridge Street in 1908 showing a solitary gig driven by a uniformed servant in a cockaded silk hat as he waits for his lady to complete her shopping. Until the appearance of the motor car, horse-drawn vehicles were the only means of transport for the better-off such as the squire, the doctor and the clergyman. The poor had no alternative but to walk unless they owned a bicycle.

Another view of Bridge Street in 1908 littered with horse-droppings, the by-product of a horse-drawn society. It was estimated that every horse deposited an average of three tons a year, perfuming the streets in summer and providing a hygiene headache for the council. Nearest the camera was William Davies's Menai Cafe at No.12, Tyrrell's drapery shop (No.10), William Rice, ironmonger (No.8), DH Pritchard's grocery store (No.6) and Chisholm's restaurant (No.4).

The Liverpool Arms, built in 1843 to cater for passengers landing from the Liverpool pleasure steamers, was one of 14 public houses in the town in 1908 and one of 5 within 100 yards of the pier gates. Pubs were a popular haunt for working men as they offered comradeship and a means of escape from overcrowded homes. But unlike today they were predominantly a male preserve and the resort of the less respectable. Although women were not barred they seldom ventured in.

August 1909. This view of Beach Road appears little different from that of today except for Evan Williams's confectionery shop at Beach House, known as West End Stores, and Owen's refreshment rooms two doors away, both of which are now private houses. Nor is there a television aerial or satellite dish to be seen, no telephone wires or even a street light. And the police station in the distance, then occupied by Inspector Owen Jones, has since been re-located.

Capel Mawr, the Calvinistic Methodist chapel built originally in 1838, rebuilt in 1856 and renovated in 1904. A 1911 Royal Commission Report on Religion in Wales concluded that the chapel had 860 adherents (50 per cent of the town population!) including 495 communicants. No fewer than 296 attended Sunday school of whom 109 were under the age of 15. A total of 14 services were held each week so people's lives were inevitably centred around the chapel.

Chapel Street in 1907, then empty of cars. Most of the houses, along with those of New Street and Brynafon Street, were built by local developers following an auction sale of land held at the Victoria Hotel in April 1880. Note the "Tea and coffee" sign outside the house on the right. The front rooms of many houses in the town were converted into temporary dining areas during the summer months to take full advantage of the commercial possibilities brought by holidaymakers.

New Street on a postcard of 1918 before ten council houses were built on the left side of the road in 1931. They cost £356 each and let to tenants at a rental of 6/- a week. Their simple, functional design provided far better facilities than anything the inhabitants had been used to in the past. This was Menai Bridge's third venture into council house building, having completed 16 houses on the gasworks field, named Rhyd Menai, in 1919 and 12 at Bro Hyfryd in 1930.

These four houses in Dale Street were demolished in 1937 and the occupants re-housed in Well Street. In 1897, before the road was widened, an ambitious proposal was made to connect Llanfairpwll with Beaumaris by means of a light electric railway running along Dale Street and High Street but the Light Railway Commissioners refused to sanction the plan as the roads were not wide enough for a railway track as well as for normal road traffic. .

This view of Hill Street in July 1907 was not unusual as people often walked in the middle of the road. By today they have learnt not to do so. The building on the right in the middle distance was the New Hall, built about 1850 by Richard Davies who later presented it to the Town Council. In the 1920s it became a cinema. Films at first were silent, accompanied by a pianist, but after 'talkies' arrived in the early 1930s they provided a popular form of public entertainment.

Children making their own fun in Well Street about 1910. Well Street was subject to a clearance order in 1934 as part of the Town Council's programme to replace substandard houses with decent homes for the working class. The houses were demolished three years later and the occupants re-housed in Bron Fedw (Mount Street) where 10 three-bedroomed and 4 two-bedroomed houses were built at an average cost of £370 each and let for 6/- and 5/- per week.

A peaceful scene in Mount Street about 1910 as the driver of this cart has the road to himself. The Wesleyan Methodist chapel was built on the site of the original meeting-house in 1859 and when a new, larger chapel was built at the lower end of Hill street in 1902 the old Mount Street building was purchased for the Menai Bridge brass band where it has remained ever since. The shop on the left was that of Thomas Pritchard, grocer, who was also described as a cooper.

The view taken from this exact position has now completely changed. The Mountain View houses are today all but obscured by the Menai Pharmacy and health centre, now built on the land in the foreground. The house in front of the terrace has disappeared while a number of new properties have since sprung up on the skyline. The card, posted in 1907, was produced by Wright & Company of Bootle and shows a family group making its way up Coronation Road to Well Street

The Square, thronged with people, during Ffair Borth in 1905. For many it was an occasion for joyful revelry but much serious shopping was also done there with money saved throughout the year. Prices were lower than in the shops and there was an opportunity to see the expanding range of manufactured goods. It was reputed to be the largest fair in north Wales, and special cheap-day tickets were offered by the railway company from Chester and other coastal towns.

The 'fun of the fair' at Ffair Borth on a postcard dated November 1919. It was the great social occasion of the year providing a good day's entertainment from the monotony of daily life and the hardships endured during the First World War. It had pedlars' stalls, boxing booths, barrel organs, fortune tellers, coconut shies, Punch and Judy, swings and sideshows of all kinds. Electricity had earlier replaced steam to power the large roundabout in the Waun field.

A fine view of the annual horse fair which was held prior to Ffair Borth on the site now occupied by the Waitrose supermarket and car park. It was an important event in the agricultural calendar and was reputed to be the best market in the country for the sale of two-year old shire-bred fillies and geldings. It enabled specialist rearers to sell stock to buyers, and had the added advantage of being easily reached by rail. Weekly livestock sales were also held there throughout the year.

Congestion on the highway as buyers and sellers congregate outside the Rock Vaults during the annual horse fair in 1907. Most sales were conducted by auction in the Mona Road livestock market but it was not unusual for horses to be sold by private treaty in the road, and it would appear that a deal was being struck for the horse on the right of the photograph. The road was the only thoroughfare into Anglesey but the horse dealers had no doubt about its proper purpose.

The Anglesey Arms Hotel, before another storey was added, on a postcard of 1905. It offered every facility for middle class family holidays, including a large garden, a tennis court and a billiard room while the adjoining stables offered 'Carriages for hire'. A week's stay during the summer months was upwards of £3. The road sweeper cleaning the highway of horse-droppings appears to be enjoying a conversation with the town postman.

The Rock Vaults public house in 1905. It was built in 1853 and during the early 1900s it was occupied by Ellis Timothy who was also a wholesale wine and spirit merchant. The building was demolished in 1969 to make way for road improvements on the busy, and at the time, the only highway into Anglesey, and was situated on what is now a large roundabout. The Anglesey Arms Hotel, before it was extensively altered, can be seen on the left.

Old Cottage, Menia Bridge.   5051 The "Wyndham" Series.

This photograph, clearly posed, was published as a postcard and sent in 1912. The cottage was 'Buarth Cerrig', later demolished to make way for the Tea Gardens (see opposite page), now replaced by a restaurant. The domestic lives of the occupants of working class cottages attracted little attention but we do know that the standard of comfort was low and that housework was a chore. Heating and cooking were by coal fire, lighting by oil lamp and washing done by hand.

Jones's Tea Gardens on Mona Road in the 1930s. A notice in the garden offers accommodation for cyclists. It was usual for guest houses to offer reduced prices for members of the Cyclists Touring Club, a national organisation for one of the most popular recreations of the inter-war years when a new bicycle could be purchased for £5. It was also a sport in which women could participate fully in order to enjoy the pleasures of the countryside.

A tranquil scene in 1908 as a family gig makes its way slowly along Mona Road which today has a relentless flow of traffic all day. Possession of one's own horse-drawn trap, in addition to being an essential form of transport, was a mark of social status. But it was not cheap to run as horses needed harnessing, feeding and stabling. The house on the left was Rose Cottage (illustrated on the opposite page) while the one in the distance was built on the site of the former Marquis Inn.

Rose Cottage, run by a Mrs Owen, was one of several guest houses in the town which catered for the upper reaches of the working class and white collar workers who could afford to pay £1.10s for a week's stay. For those of lesser means there were a number of lodging houses offering accommodation for as little as £1 a week. The postcard, dated 1912, was produced by the owner to advertise her business. Perhaps this card was one of those displayed for sale outside her door.

The Bryntirion Restaurant was one of several cafes catering for visitors who arrived during the summer months either as day-trippers on the pleasure steamers or as holidaymakers staying for a week or two. Note the Fry's and Cadbury's adverts in the window and on the enamelled signs. Chocolate and cocoa were once luxury products but were now within the grasp of a large section of society. The Bryntirion later became known as the Bridge End Cafe. It is now Tafarn y Bont.

The Victoria Hotel before the First World War. It was built in 1852 when seaside holidays were becoming popular among the well-to-do and Menai Bridge was attracting visitors arriving by the Liverpool steamers. The hotel boasted "Hot and cold baths and a capital billiard room" and was one of the first subscribers in the town to have a telephone (Tel. No.9). Bed & breakfast cost 4/-, a week's stay was £3 and "special arrangements offered Saturday to Monday".

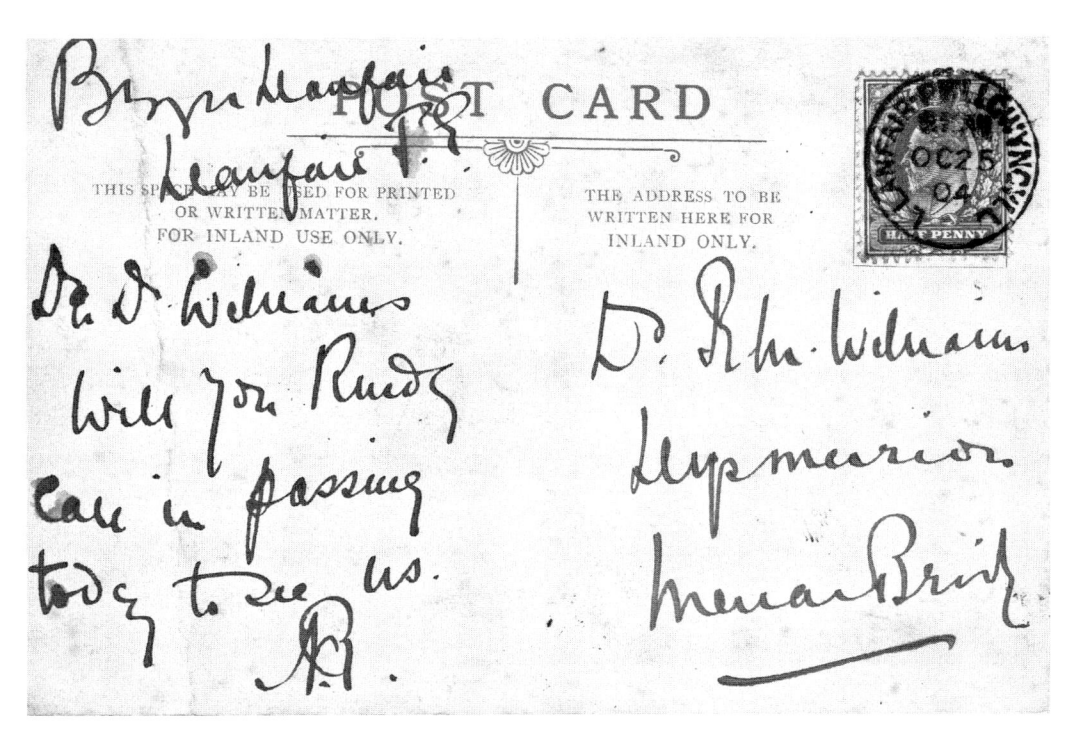

This postcard epitomizes the fine service provided by the Post Office during the Edwardian era. Postage on letters was still a penny, having remained unchanged since 1840. Postcards could be sent for ½d and would reach their destination the next morning while local ones arrived later the same day. This card was posted in Llanfairpwll at 8.00 am requesting Dr Williams to "call today" and it would have reached his surgery in Menai Bridge by the second (afternoon) delivery.

EY 268, a smart two-seater car owned by Dr RM Williams outside his surgery in Water Street in 1913 where he served as a family doctor until his early death in 1920 at the age of 53. Prior to his first car in 1912 Dr Williams did his rounds in a horse-drawn gig, and he could not have imagined or foreseen the total disruption in the pattern of life by the arrival of motor transport. No other single influence since the Industrial Revolution made a greater impact on society.

John Gresty shows off his new motor car during the late 1920s. There were very few garages at this time so it was not unusual for drivers to carry a spare can of petrol (seen on the car's running board). The inter-war years witnessed a huge expansion of private car ownership with small family cars coming within the reach of the middle class for whom they became a status symbol. John Gresty later acquired the William Roberts timber yard before passing it on to his son Eric.

The pride of ownership is written all over this photograph. Charles Ringrose, landlord of the Cambria Inn, stands proudly alongside his new motor cycle, EY 391, a 3½ horse-power BSA with a wicker sidecar, shortly after it was first registered in June 1913 Motor cycles were becoming popular as a cheaper alternative to the motor car. Production increased rapidly during the First World War and by 1920 there were more motor cycles than cars on British roads.

A mixed class in the old National School in Mona Road (the present Telford Centre) with their headmaster, George Senogles, in 1924. It was built in 1853 at a cost of £469. Education was compulsory for 5 to 10 year olds, and it was not until 1918 that the school-leaving age was raised to 14. Teaching was monotonous and factual with reliance on the repetitive learning of tables and passages from scripture. Discipline was rigorous and the cane was an ever present threat.

Westbury Mount where the Rev Evan Cynffig Davies ran a private grammar school from 1875 until 1908. It catered for both boarders and day scholars, including mature students being prepared for the universities and for the ministry. Davies was a remarkable man. In addition to being the minister of the Independent chapels in both Menai Bridge and Llanfairpwll, he was a biographer and a musician. The house is now part of the University's School of Ocean Sciences.

A squad of Anglesey Volunteer Reserves parading in Dale Street during the First World War before (perhaps) marching to Church Island for the military funeral of a local serviceman (see opposite page). The building behind was the second elementary school to be built in the town (in 1865) having previously been held in temporary accommodation in the New Hall in Hill Street. The new school had a small playing field behind with a headmaster's house later built alongside.

A Menai Bridge casualty of the First World War is buried in Church Island with full military honours led by the Anglesey Volunteers and accompanied by the *Clio* boys band and a group of wounded servicemen probably from the Bodlondeb convalescent home. Unfortunately there are no notes on the back of the postcard to indicate the date or the identity of the soldier who had been returned home but failed to recover from wounds sustained whilst on active service.

A group of wounded servicemen at Bodlondeb, a large house on the mainland near the suspension bridge, the home of Henry Rees Davies. During World War I, whilst the owner was serving with his Regiment in France, Bodlondeb was turned over as a VAD convalescent home under the command of Mrs John Davies of 'Ceris', but still under military control. It was staffed by Red Cross nurses with the help of middle class women with time on their hands.

Penhesgyn, an open-air sanatorium for children suffering from tuberculosis. It was opened in 1910 and run by the King Edward VII Welsh National Memorial Association. The sanatorium had accommodation for 16 girls, with a school provided on the site, but due to a decline in the incidence of tuberculosis the hospital was closed in 1958. The postcard shows some of the young patients on the balcony as the principal cure was sunlight, fresh air and plenty of rest.

Menai Bridge brass band c.1897 with George Senogles, the bandmaster, standing in the centre of the back row. The band was formed in 1894 and made its first public appearance during Queen Victoria's Diamond Jubilee celebrations 3 years later. Military style uniforms were purchased in 1899 and a former chapel in Mount Street, purchased for £150 in 1903, was used for rehearsals (see page 84). During the next few years the band played on the promenade on summer evenings.

Menai Bridge Miniature Rifle Club was formed in 1914. An outdoor range was secured on land beside the Llanfairpwll road and in 1915 an indoor range was built alongside it so that practice could continue throughout the winter. Competitions were held against other local clubs as well as between members. From 1916 members of the Volunteer Training Corps joined in order to practice their marksmanship before enlisting in the RWF. The club was disbanded in 1920.

Menai Bridge Lawn Tennis Club. 1913.

Members of the Tennis Club pose proudly for the camera in 1913. It was a private club from which the lower orders were totally excluded because of the cost of equipment and an annual subscription of 10/6d for men and 7/6d for ladies. Temporary membership was also available to visitors at 2/6d a week. Like golf, tennis was a middle class game and viewed as 'sissified' by working men until public courts started opening in the 1930s. The game then spread widely.

Members and guests of the Tennis Club gather for the official opening of a second court in 1903. It was situated on the Holyhead Road on the site now occupied by the telephone exchange. Tennis was one of the few sports in which women could participate but they were handicapped by playing in long sweeping skirts. Even for men it was a social rather than a competitive game, played with only moderate exertion with less emphasis on pace and more on placing the ball.

Menai Bridge Football Club, 1911-12, with the North Wales Junior Cup which they won again in 1914. By the end of November of that year eight of the team had volunteered for active service. Football flourished during the Edwardian era and was played by boys in every street. Most villages fielded a team and the local papers gave graphic accounts of matches. It had become an exciting spectator sport in which supporters felt themselves passionately involved in their team.

As Menai Bridge had no sandy beach to compete with the north Wales resorts of Llandudno, Rhyl and Colwyn Bay, the Town Council developed Carreg-yr-Halen into a bathing place for visitors but it was widely used by townsfolk as well. Thirty bathing huts were later erected and an attendant hired to collect fees for their use. This postcard was sent by a holidaymaker in 1931.

Members of the town Fire Brigade resplendent in their new uniforms and helmets in 1911, ready to man the new horse-drawn fire engine purchased that year at a cost of £385.

Standing (*Left to right*): John Owen, R.J Jones, Albert Rowlands, W. Morgan Jones, Owen Thomas (Captain)

Seated: J.R Owen, Owen Evans, R.L Williams

Fire "Cartrefle" July 10 1917

An unknown photographer was quickly on the scene of a disastrous fire at Cartrefle on 10th July 1917. The house, occupied by the Turner family and standing just off the Holyhead Road, was well ablaze before the arrival of the fire engine. As there was no mains water pipe within half-a-mile of the property it was impossible to save the house and it was completely destroyed. But the owner still had to pay the standard charge of £3.18s for the services of the Fire Brigade.

Cadnant woollen mill in 1908. Established during the 1840s it was run by John Morgan & Sons and employed several weavers. Power was obtained from the River Cadnant which was fed into a storage pond with sufficient water to drive a large wheel but steam power was used during periods of dry weather. Cadnant was a hive of activity during the Edwardian years. In addition to the mill it housed a factory making writing-slates for schools as well as a smithy and a shop.

John Morris at work in his smithy at Cadnant in 1909 with Owen Hughes, a 'gwas' at Bryn Meurig, Llandegfan, looking on. Shoeing horses was only part of the blacksmith's trade. He also made and repaired all kinds of ironwork, from tools and implements to gates and wagon parts. John Morris was one of 216 blacksmiths in Anglesey in 1911 but after 1920 their number dwindled sharply. His was one of the last to survive in the county before closure in 1980.

The Moorings, a fine detached villa in Cadnant, was the residence of Hugh Bulkeley Price, a director of the North & South Wales Bank which merged with the Midland Bank in 1908. His income and his comfortable style of living placed him in the so-called middle class with a well-defined place in the social hierarchy. He took full advantage of the availability of a plentiful supply of domestic servants by employing a live-in housekeeper, a cook and a housemaid.

August 1905. Menai Ville, a fine terrace of houses erected on the former site of four old cottages known as 'The Barracks', built to accommodate men working on the suspension bridge. The occupants were the better-off, with most being enumerated in the 1901 Census as "living on their means" with at least one domestic servant. In winter there would have been smoke coming from every chimney as coal fires were needed for cooking and heating, unless gas had been installed.